W9-AVP-993

The Sexual Abuse of Children and Adolescents

The Sexual Abuse of Children and Adolescents

Margaret O. Hyde and
Elizabeth H. Forsyth, M.D.

The Millbrook Press
Brookfield, Connecticut

To Andrea Schaffner, M.D.

Library of Congress Cataloging-in-Publication Data
Hyde, Margaret O. (Margaret Oldroyd).
The sexual abuse of children and adolescents / Margaret O. Hyde and
Elizabeth H. Forsyth.
p. cm.
Includes bibliographical references and index.
Summary: Covers the history of sexual abuse of children, effects on children,
profiles of abusers, controversies surrounding the Internet, Megan's law, and
repressed and false memories.
ISBN 0-7613-0058-9 (lib. bdg.)
1. Child sexual abuse—United States—Juvenile literature. 2. Child
molesters—United States—Juvenile literature. 3. Sexually abused children—
United States—Juvenile literature. [1. Child sexual abuse.] I. Forsyth,
Elizabeth Held. II. Title.
HV6570.2.H93   1997
362.7´6´0973—dc20   96–36366   CIP   AC

Published by The Millbrook Press, Inc.
2 Old New Milford Road
Brookfield, Connecticut 06804

CONTENTS

THE SEXUAL ABUSE OF CHILDREN AND ADOLESCENTS

CHAPTER ONE

A NEW LOOK AT AN OLD SECRET

Most children and adolescents never suffer sexual abuse, but for those who do, the emotional problems that it causes can be devastating.[1]

By definition, the sexual abuse of children occurs when someone imposes sexual behavior on a young person who may not understand what is happening. The abuse is usually taking place against the younger person's will. Child sexual abuse victims range in age from infancy to adolescence. Some reports indicate that one third to one half of the victims are under the age of seven.[2] According to one report, adolescents are victims in 71 percent of all proven reports of sexual abuse.[3]

In recent years, there has been an increased awareness of sexual abuse, which is making victims of thousands of young people. Society is no longer blaming the victim for sexual abuse, but is attempting to understand the complex factors that cause it and the importance of educating people of all ages about it. The silence that surrounded the issue is being broken, and people are beginning to understand that the prevention of sexual abuse is everyone's responsibility. The problem of sexual abuse of children and adolescents is receiving world attention. In the summer of 1996, delegates from 122 countries met in Sweden to seek solutions to the growing problems of child prostitution, trafficking, and pornography.

In most reported cases of child sexual abuse, only sexual contact is included. However, any of the following are types of sexual abuse: fondling, the touching of sexual organs, anal or oral sex, intercourse, pornography, indecent exposure, obscene telephone calls, ceremonies in which children are exposed or used sexually, allowing children to witness sex acts between adults, and prostitution.

Many experts believe that sexual abuse is the most underreported form of child maltreatment because of the "conspiracy of silence" that so often characterizes these cases. Very young children simply lack the verbal ability to tell of conduct that is inappropriate or crimi-

MYTH *Rape is the only kind of sexual abuse.*

FACT *There are many types of sexual abuse, including making obscene comments or showing pornography to a child. Anytime a perpetrator forces, manipulates, or tricks an individual who is less powerful or has less understanding, the activity is defined as abuse.*

nal, and older children are often threatened into silence. Often when children and adolescents do confide in trusted adults, their reports are dismissed as fantasy or lies.

In 1979, one of the first studies of the incidence of child sexual abuse in the general population indicated that 20 percent of females and 9 percent of males had been sexually abused before their eighteenth birthdays. Since then, estimates of the incidence of child sexual abuse have varied widely, ranging from 1 in 100 cases to 1 in 3. Among the reasons for the variance in the numbers of reported cases is the changing definition of sexual abuse, the ages of the persons polled, and the time that has elapsed since the incident. For example, young children are more open to suggestion than older children or adults, and may alter a memory or begin to believe that something happened that did not. Research has also shown that people's memories of events can change or be reinterpreted over time.[4]

Studies show that 15 to 38 percent of all adult women and about 10 percent of all men report that they were sexually abused during childhood and adolescence.[5] About one third of the adults who report they were sexually abused as children were victimized by older children, such as cousins or siblings.[6] The sexual abuse of boys is thought to be more rarely reported than that of girls, perhaps because boys are less willing to admit that they are victims.[7]

ABUSE WITHIN FAMILIES
Sexual abuse by relatives is often kept secret, ignored, and even condoned by some of the family members. As a result, many incest cases—cases in which the abuser is related by blood or by marriage—have been, and still

are, undetected. Even when mothers have spoken out to protect their children from incestuous behavior, many have not been believed.[8]

Children are warned to stay away from strangers, but little is usually said about abuse within a family. Few people are comfortable talking about such a difficult subject. It is hard enough to think of the possibility of strangers molesting children, but incest is unthinkable for most adults.

Today, research suggests that 50 to 90 percent of sexual abuse involves family members.[9] This percentage is only an estimate, however, because most cases of incestuous sexual abuse are not reported. Most children are afraid to tell about abuse within the family for a number of reasons—including threats of violence, which may be real.

Even without such threats, in some cases a child may be reluctant to tell about abuse. Some children worry about who will provide for the family if the offender is punished and imprisoned. A child who is victimized by a parent may hate the abusive experiences, but still love the offender. Some may even believe that the behavior is an acceptable form of loving. An older child may also be silent and endure sexual abuse by a parent to protect a younger sibling from the experience. Often that child later discovers that the sibling was also being abused, despite the attempt to protect him or her.

A NEW LIGHT

Many children suffer from sexual abuse year after year in helpless silence. No matter what their age or gender, many victims of sexual abuse believe that they are the only ones to whom this form of abuse has happened. Increasingly, however, movies, television programs, and newspaper reports (including headlines about sexual abuse on the Internet) are making the problem of sexual abuse more visible and increasing people's awareness. Few things provoke more public outrage than sex crimes against children.[10] Many community groups and schools include programs about how to avoid sexual abuse. For example, the Boy Scouts teach children the three Rs: recognize, resist, and report anyone who attempts to use young people's normal curiosity about sex as an opportunity to attempt sexual abuse.[11] Many teachers include discussions of sexual abuse as part of social studies or health classes.

Although most incidents of sexual abuse may remain untold, many young children who have learned the difference between "good and bad touching" are willing to tell adults about their problems. Adolescents who have learned what sexual abuse is tend to be more willing to tell trusted adults. A major factor in the prevention of child abuse is teaching children to report any sexual victimization, and teaching adults to listen to children in order to help keep them safe. Because of the increase in awareness and education about sexual abuse, many victims are more willing to ask for help, and more help is available to them.

CHAPTER TWO

FROM THE ANCIENTS TO THE INTERNET

Sexual abuse of children was more common in early times than it is today. In most cultures, abusive practices that would not be tolerated today were the norm.[1] Throughout much of history, children were regarded as having no rights and deserving of no respect.

The custom of abandoning children was widespread and widely accepted by civil and church authorities from ancient times through the Middle Ages. In many large families the abandoning of babies was a matter of survival. Families were large, and food and housing were scarce. Many abandoned children who did not die from exposure and starvation were used as servants and prostitutes and were constantly threatened with severe abuse from adults.[2]

Ancient attitudes about children differed in other ways as well. The virginity of girls was extremely important in Biblical times, although a girl under three legally retained her virginity no matter how often she was sexually penetrated by a male. Intercourse with a female baby was not illegal.[3] If a daughter was raped, her father could demand monetary compensation from the offender and could hire her out for sex again.[4] A girl's consent to sex was of no value, since she was considered the property of her father.

In Biblical times, boys received full adult status at age thirteen, but before that age they were classified with women and slaves and were therefore subject to sexual abuse. The rape of a male under the age of nine was not punishable. In the Hebrew laws, a daughter who gave herself to a man without her father's permission was considered a harlot, but if she sold her body with her father's consent, she was not an outcast.[5]

Males and females growing up in Greece and Rome were often used sexually.[6] Boy brothels thrived from the sixth to the fourth centuries B.C.[7] The castration of boys to make them eunuch servants was also a big business in ancient times, and castrated children were considered sexually attractive.[8] Eunuchs were also in demand as singers during the Middle Ages and later.[9]

Before the thirteenth century, sexual activity with a very young person was not legally considered rape. Sex play between children and adults was common even in the Middle Ages.[10] Sexual abuse, whipping, and battering of the young by their caretakers were considered acceptable behavior.

By the sixteenth century, childhood began to be considered a distinct phase of human development. With the exception of the Christ child, children were seldom depicted in the arts before this time. The invention of the printing press, the increase of adult literacy, and the educational and social work of Jesuit priests all helped to develop the idea of the innocence of children and the need to protect them.

Although the widespread sexual misuse of many children continued into the eighteenth and nineteenth centuries, children were more highly valued, and their education became an important concern. Still, some children were sent out to brothels by their parents. In America and England in the Victorian era, although the discussion of sex was suppressed by "proper" people, there was a great deal of clandestine sexual activity and pornography.[11] Poor girls and boys, ages ten to eighteen, frequently became prostitutes. In 1885, the British Parliament passed legislation protecting women and children from prostitution.[12] In 1874, the Society for the Protection of Children was formed in New York City.[13]

Before laws were passed to protect children, and even for some years afterward, sex merchants sold "involuntary prostitutes" in a lively trade known as "white slavery." They worked in local, national, and international markets. Abductors stalked playgrounds, schools, and recreation centers, seducing curious children and taking them to strange cities where they were powerless to escape. After they were sexually abused, girls were told they had lost their character and that no one would take them in. If they ran away, they usually returned within a week, because they had no place to go for food and shelter.[14] Boys, too, sold sexual favors to survive, and many of them suffered low self-esteem and other emotional problems as a result.

By the end of the nineteenth century, a number of individuals and organizations became advocates for children who were sold into sexual slavery. The League of Nations, and later the United Nations, took measures against the international trafficking of women and children. In America, the Mann Act was passed in 1912, making the interstate transportation of women and children for immoral purposes a crime. But, despite these efforts, the child sex trade continued in America and around the world. [15]

In the culture of the Western world in the early twentieth century, children were no longer considered property. The concept of seeking the best interests of the child came into being. Although this new attitude improved the conditions of many young people, hundreds of thousands of children are still involved in the sex industry in the United States and abroad. Some are sold into the sex trade by their families. Others are kidnapped or lured by traffickers with offers of domestic work or other employment. These victims often then find themselves in foreign lands without money, unable to speak the language, and with no way out but to cooperate with their abductors.

Although the incidence of child sexual abuse continues, twentieth-century society has a greatly increased intolerance for it and a greater willingness to tackle this problem.[16] Legal measures are being taken against citizens who travel abroad to engage in sex acts with children, acts that are illegal in their own countries. A growing network of religious and human rights organizations has been making progress in exposing the

---

MYTH *Incest is a family matter; fathers and stepfathers can do whatever they please with their children.*

FACT *Incest is illegal.*

---

international sex trade and assisting its victims. One organization, the campaign to End Child Prostitution in Asian Tourism (ECPAT) was founded in 1990, and has offices in twenty-eight countries.[17]

CHILD PORNOGRAPHY

Child pornography is defined as any visual or written depiction, on film or in print, of the sexual abuse of children. Today, every state in the United States has laws that prohibit adults from engaging in sexual conduct with children and adolescents. The Protection of Children Against Sexual Exploitation Act, passed in 1977, prohibits the participation of children in obscene performances, the transportation for purposes of sale of materials depicting children in sexual conduct, and the interstate transportation of children for purposes of prostitution or obscene performances.[18]

Despite this act, several hundred magazines, international mailing lists, videotapes, and other forms of child pornography are still being sold. Producers find a steady supply of actresses and actors for their "kiddy porn" on the streets where runaways and throwaways search for money to provide themselves with food and shelter. In some cases, parents sell the services of their children, or use them as models in their own pornographic productions.

Child sex rings are also illegal in the United States. Sex rings are defined as having one or more offenders sexually involved simultaneously with several child victims. Sex rings are not necessarily motivated by the opportunity for financial gain. For example, when a teacher was convicted of sexually molesting several of his students, he was considered to have operated a sex ring. Although group sex is involved in some cases, it is more likely that the offender is interacting with the children one at a time. In some cases, the children may know each other, but many times the victims are unaware that the offender is having sex with others and therefore feel that they are special to the abuser.

The Internet has created a new version of child sexual abuse. Since 1993, the FBI has been investigating the use of computer technology to exploit children. In 1995, a dozen people in the United States were arrested for using America Online to exchange digitized photographs of young children posing naked or engaged in sex.[19]

There is considerable controversy about ways to prevent child pornography on the Internet, as well as other forms of sexual abuse, such as luring children to meet offenders via bulletin boards. Some services, as well as their subscribers, are making ongoing efforts to help prevent the use of the Internet to transmit indecent material.

The Communications Decency Act of 1996 made it a felony to transmit material on the Internet that was not suitable for young people to see or read. This act

MYTH *Victims of sex offenses are attractive young women.*

FACT *Victims can be any age and either sex. Many rape victims are under the age of nine, but they may be infants, they may be elderly, or any age in between.*

began a battle around the issues of free speech and the legality of the government's attempts to monitor the Internet. Many critics of the law believe that there are better ways to keep children away from electronic pornography. They believe that parents, not the government, should be in control of what is suitable for children. Some Internet services, however, such as America Online, Prodigy, and CompuServe, provide screening and new types of software designed to protect kids from sexually explicit material.

Defining the term *indecent* is just one of the problems with providing online safety for children. No solution has yet been found that is 100 percent effective in controlling data on the Internet. So while governments, schools, and special interest groups struggle to find ways to rid the network of pornographic data, much of the responsibility for protection against electronic forms of sexual abuse falls on the parents and young people using the Internet.

CHAPTER THREE

WHO ARE THE ABUSERS?

Little is known about the people who sexually abuse children. There has not been enough research, and the surveyed samples are small and do not always include all the types of abusers. In addition, the definitions of abuse vary from study to study.[1]

In the past, experts believed that most of the abusers were strangers to the victims and that the victims were mainly female. No one realized that abuse could have severe long-term effects on the victims. Research done in the 1980s and 1990s, however, suggests that almost all abusers are males who are known to the victims, and that most abuse occurs within the family. According to some research studies, 99 percent of the perpetrators were known to the child, and 62 percent were biological fathers or other father figures.[2]

Abusers can be found in every type of social, economic, and professional circumstance. They may behave normally in every other way. Most sexual abusers are not mentally ill, and most do not physically harm their victims. Most abusers are not gay; the majority are heterosexual (attracted to members of the opposite sex).[3] Many are married and have children. There are no special characteristics that apply to all abusers, except that they are sexually attracted to children and have a tendency to act on their attractions.

Several studies have been done in attempts to identify the reasons why abusers act as they do. Various factors may increase the likelihood that an abuser will act out abusive behavior. These include family situations, life crises, personality type, and the use of alcohol or illegal drugs, which weaken a person's ability to control behavior. When under the influence of alcohol or drugs, people lose their inhibitions and often behave in ways they might not normally behave.

Some abusers have serious mental illnesses. A small number are violent individuals, and have committed other serious crimes, although this is not typical of child molesters. These violent offenders are the ones whose horrible deeds receive the most publicity in the media. Some abusers may stalk and then abduct a child forcibly, and in some cases the end result is murder—especially if the offender panics and fears being discovered.[4]

Most abusers can be described as having an antisocial personality. They have little regard for the rights of other people. Such people do not conform to socially acceptable standards of behavior. They feel little or no remorse or guilt about their behavior because their conscience is underdeveloped.

Most sex offenders appear to lack empathy, the ability to imagine how they would feel if they were in the victim's situation. Some of these abusers are sadists, people who enjoy overpowering and causing harm to a weaker person.

In contrast, other child abuse offenders abhor violence. They are nonassertive individuals, who often feel generally inferior or inadequate, have low self-esteem, poor social skills, and a great need for acceptance. Rather than use physical force, they are kind and persuasive. They attempt to form a trusting relationship with their victims, using money, gifts, friendship, or other privileges as enticement. In addition to sexual gratification, these abusers appear to be seeking love and acceptance, needs that may never have been satisfied by their parents. Some researchers have described the members of many abusers' families as isolated from one another, rigid, authoritarian, and lacking in warmth toward their children.[5] In one study, one third of the offenders were victims of sexual or physical abuse or emotional abuse or physical neglect at home.[6]

Child molesters are sometimes divided into two groups: incest offenders and pedophiles. Incest is defined as sexual contact between individuals who are biologically related (for example, a father and daughter, grandparent and grandchild, or brother and sister) or between stepparents and stepchildren. The term *pedophile* refers to a person sixteen years or older who experiences intense, recurring urges, fantasies, or behavior involving sexual activity with a child or children who have not yet reached puberty—usually younger than age thirteen.

INCEST ABUSERS

No one really knows how extensive incest is in the United States because many cases are not reported. As noted earlier, 62 percent of known offenders were fathers or surrogate fathers of the victims. In one study, 1 percent of adult women surveyed reported having had sexual contact with their fathers or stepfathers; other estimates range from 7 percent to 38 percent of the population of the United States.[7] Brother-sister incest may be more common than most people realize, according to some experts, but father-daughter incest may be reported more frequently.[8]

Many offender fathers are motivated by the need for power and domination. They suffer from what Dr. William E. Prendergast calls the King-of-the-Castle syndrome; they have an exaggerated need to control, and

---

MYTH *It is wise to ignore sexual abuse when it happens in the family in order to prevent angry reactions from family members.*

FACT *Sexual abuse is always harmful, and the abused person needs to tell a responsible person and get help.*

---

they hold distorted ideas about male and female roles, believing that men should be dominant and women should be submissive. Such an individual may have difficulty relating to adult women, and may displace his wife with a daughter that he uses as a sexual object. Many of these men are outwardly normal and socially charming, but their secret life at home is very different. Some of these fathers may use physical force.[9]

Some abusive fathers use psychological, rather than physical, force. When abuse begins at an early age, the incestuous father is able to indoctrinate the victim, telling her that she is his favorite, giving her love and affection, and making her promise to keep their special secret. He is often very possessive, and he may forbid her to have boyfriends.

Although pedophiles and incest offenders have commonly been regarded as two distinct types of abusers, recent studies cast doubt on this idea. New information shows that many incest offenders also abuse children outside their homes. In a study of 159 incestuous fathers of girls, 49 percent had abused unrelated girls, 12 percent had abused unrelated boys, and 19 percent had raped adult women.[10]

PEDOPHILES

Some pedophiles are attracted to males, some to females, and others to both. Pedophiles who are attracted to females usually prefer eight- to ten-year-olds, who have not reached puberty. Offenders who are attracted to children past puberty are sometimes termed *hebephiles.* Some pedophiles engage in sexual activities with adults and children. Many pedophiles choose professions and activities that give them opportunities for contact with children.

There was nothing unusual about Mr. P. He was a married man with two children; he had a good job, was respected in the community, and volunteered as a Boy Scout troop leader. He often spoke proudly of his role in helping and befriending boys from disadvantaged homes; he took them on camping and fishing trips and to ball games. Everyone in town was shocked when it was discovered that he was engaging in sexual activities with several scouts in his troop. He admitted that he had felt attracted to young boys since he was a teenager, and had become involved with more than a dozen boys over a period of ten years. But Mr. P. did not see anything wrong in what he had been doing, and he denied that his behavior was sexually abusive. He believed that he was giving love and caring attention to these boys. He also believed that he was educating them about sex.

Mr. P.'s thinking is typical of that of many sex offenders. Their beliefs allow them to continue abusing while rationalizing their behavior as something other than what it really is. In contrast to Mr. P., who genuinely believed he was helping the boys he abused, other offenders recognize that they are taking advantage of their victims, but they cannot resist the urge to have sex with a child. They may feel disgusted and remorseful, and may even resolve to stop, but they continue to repeat the same pattern.

CHILDREN AS ABUSERS

According to many authorities, child sexual abuse should be considered an addiction that often begins early in life. Adolescent boys are known to be responsible for as much as 50 percent of child sexual abuse.

> MYTH *Children never become sexual offenders until after they reach adolescence.*
>
> FACT *Young children who were sexually abused may become abusers as young as age five.*

More than half of adult sex offenders committed their first crime before they were eighteen years old.[11] The pattern may begin in late childhood or early adolescence, when the potential abuser begins to imagine having sex with younger children. Eventually, the abuser starts to act out the fantasies.[12]

It is not rare to find children as young as age seven who sexually abuse other children. According to the FBI, young sex offenders should always be considered past or current victims of sexual abuse, because sexually aggressive behavior is often a sign that the abuser himself has been victimized. Because of increasing concern about these offenders, Colorado amended its Child Protection Law in 1991 to mandate the reporting of children under ten years old who are sexually aggressive toward other children.[13]

Experts agree that in sexual abuse cases, there is usually an age difference of five years between the victim and abuser and the abuser uses some kind of force. When very young children are involved, there may be little or no difference in age or size, and the children may appear to be equals. But in reality, one may be more powerful than the other.[14]

Eight-year-old Willie was a very quiet, shy boy—a follower who found it difficult to say no to anyone. Everyone thought that he and his classmate Ken were just friends. But no one realized that Ken, the most popular kid in the class and the best player on the soccer team, had been secretly luring Willie into playing sex games. Willie wasn't sure that he wanted to continue, but after the first time it happened, Ken threatened to tell if Willie refused. Although the boys were the same age, Ken was obviously an abuser.

Some sexual behavior among children is simply exploratory, and not abusive. For example, young boys may inspect and compare penises, simply showing normal curiosity about their bodies. Curiosity and touching among preschoolers are generally considered normal behaviors, as is joking about sex in all age groups.

Some adults, however, believe that children should not be exposed to any sexual information and should not engage in any sexual behavior. They do not want to face the fact that children are born with sexuality,

---

MYTH *Sexual abuse is the result of alcohol or other drug abuse.*

FACT *Although many sex offenders have problems with alcohol and other drugs, these are neither the cause nor an excuse for a sex offense. Treating the chemical problem will not necessarily affect the sexual problem.*

---

and they are not aware of what normal sexual development is. They may ignore behavior that is sexually aggressive and allow it to continue. Some do not believe that very young children can be abusers, nor do they realize that the behavior is harmful. At the other end of the spectrum, there are a small number of people who think it is okay for adults to have sex with consenting young children.

Part of the problem in attempting to draw the line between normal and abusive behavior is that there is little agreement about what is normal, abnormal, or aggressive regarding the sexual behavior of young children. According to Dr. Hendrika B. Cantwell, normal is what is tolerated at home, in the classroom, on the playground, or in the neighborhood.[15]

WOMEN AS ABUSERS

Although only a small percentage of abusers are female, recently there have been increasingly frequent reports of women who have seduced their teenage sons or acquaintances. Brenda was a single mother who encouraged her teenage son to invite his friends to their house. She especially liked thirteen-year-old Jeff, and found reasons for him to visit when no one else was around. Brenda always seemed interested in everything Jeff told her, and he felt flattered by the attention she gave him. After they had known each other for a while, the meetings went beyond conversation, and progressed to touching and then to sexual intercourse. Jeff began to feel very uncomfortable about the secret he and Brenda shared, so he finally told his parents about it. When Brenda was confronted by the investigator, she admitted to having seduced Jeff. She said that he was different from all the adult men in her life; he was kind and understanding and did not abuse or betray her, as her adult lovers had done in previous relationships.

There is disagreement about the actual number of women who molest children. In one study of convicted rapists, one half of those who had experienced childhood sexual abuse said they had been abused by women.[16] This does not mean, however, that all boys who are abused by women become rapists when they are adults. Despite the claims made by these convicted offenders, some experts believe that the stories of having been abused in childhood by mothers or other women are fantasies or lies. Other experts think people are reluctant to believe that women are capable of such abuse, and as a result, these offenses may be ignored or tolerated and underreported.

A female high school teacher was charged with having had sex with three male students under age fifteen, but a jury found her innocent. The father of one boy did not find anything wrong with the teacher's behavior. He thought his son was fortunate to have had a sexual experience with an older woman.[17]

All sex abusers use similar excuses and lies to explain their behavior. Some even insist that their victims seduced them. For his or her own gratification and by means of outright violence or more subtle coercion, every child abuser takes advantage of those who are younger, less knowledgeable, and less powerful.

CHAPTER FOUR

NOT IN MY NEIGHBORHOOD

On a summer day in 1994, seven-year-old Megan Kanka of Hamilton Township, New Jersey, went across the street to look at a puppy, and she never came home. She was raped and murdered by a man who had been convicted twice for sex offenses. He had spent six years in Avenel, a New Jersey prison for sexual offenders, after molesting and attempting to murder a little girl. Megan's family was unaware of his past, however, when he moved to the neighborhood.

Spurred by anger and sympathy, a thousand people held a vigil near Megan's home after she was murdered, and more than two hundred thousand people signed a petition demanding that officials notify communities when a sexual offender moves into the area. The state lawmakers acted quickly, and within a few months after the murder, Governor Christine Todd Whitman signed a series of bills aimed at protecting communities from sex offenders; these bills became known as Megan's Law.

Megan's Law provides for setting up a registry of sex offenders and notifying police, schools, community organizations, and in some cases, adjacent neighbors, when a released offender moves into the area. According to a list of guidelines, offenders are classified according to the likelihood that they will offend again.

Megan's story and the passage of the New Jersey law named for her triggered changes in the laws of many other states around the country. By the spring of 1996, the entire country, except for Massachusetts and the District of Columbia, had laws requiring sex offenders to register with authorities. Many states also required notification of people in the community.[1] In May 1996, President Clinton signed federal legislation based on Megan's Law that requires states to warn community members when convicted sex offenders are released from prison and move into the neighborhood.[2]

But problems arose. These laws allowed notification of too many people, with the result that names, addresses, descriptions, and license-plate numbers of released child molesters became public knowledge throughout the community. People in several communities where prior offenders were planning to live dem-

---

MYTH *Sexual assaults only happen at night and only in "high risk" neighborhoods.*

FACT *Sexual assaults can occur at any time and in any place.*

---

onstrated in the streets with the rallying cry of NIMBY—"Not in My Backyard."

Carl DeFlumer was a convicted murderer and sex offender who had spent forty-two of his sixty-two years in prison. When he was paroled, he was supposed to live in New York with his sister. But his sister's neighbors learned of the plan, and they protested so angrily that she changed her mind. The State Division of Parole then decided to place DeFlumer in a halfway house, but even the ten halfway houses he applied to in New York City shunned him because he was a former sex offender.[3]

Throughout the country, a number of acts of vigilantism took place after people in the community were notified of released offenders. In one instance, two men broke into a house and beat up a man they mistook for the sex offender who lived there. In another incident, the house of a soon-to-be released convict was burned by an arsonist after police distributed flyers that described him as a sadist who had fantasies about murdering children.[4]

Several parts of Megan's Law as it was originally written were challenged in the courts. One federal judge compared the notification process to the ancient practice of branding criminals. The Constitution of the United States says that states cannot change the legal consequences of a crime after it has been committed. The judge ruled that the notification process was additional punishment for those who had been convicted and sentenced before the law took effect.[5]

The New Jersey State Supreme Court limited the community notification to cases of offenders who were considered high risk. The court said that the law infringed on their right to privacy, which is guaranteed by the Constitution. A ban on community notification in New Jersey was imposed by a federal appeals court until a decision was made on the constitutionality of the statute. So in the summer of 1996, Megan's Law was still in limbo.[6]

Some experts are especially disturbed about laws in several states that allow the continued confinement of sex offenders, even after they have served their prison terms, if a panel finds them likely to commit more crimes. In Washington State, for example, a rapist who completed his ten-year prison sentence was kept confined because prosecutors decided he was still too dangerous to be free. They sought a court hearing to have him committed to a prison for dangerous child molesters and rapists, even though he had completed a two-year treatment program during his prison term.[7]

Professor John La Fond of Seattle University School of Law says that this is "lifetime preventive detention masquerading as involuntary psychiatric treatment." He thinks it sets a dangerous precedent, because it could be extended to other types of criminal offenders.[8] The laws have been challenged in the courts based on the argument that the Constitution protects people against being tried twice for the same crime.

Experts agree that some offenders are too dangerous to be released from prison, but most sex offenders will eventually be released into the community. The new laws undoubtedly save some children, but no one knows how effective they are in making communities safer. One problem is that no one can predict dangerousness with certainty.

Badly planned community notification programs may hinder the chances for rehabilitation of less dangerous offenders. If everyone in the community recognizes a released offender, he may be shunned and isolated, and he may feel worse about himself and hopeless about changing his past behavior. He may move to a place where he is unknown, avoid treatment, and start molesting children again.

Only a small fraction of the offenders who sexually abuse children are violent, sadistic criminals, but their stories cause tremendous outrage and a demand for harsher laws and longer prison sentences. A storm of controversy has arisen about ways to balance the conflict between the issues of community safety and the rights of individuals. How can society protect people from dangerous predators without violating the rights of those who have already been punished for their crimes?

POTENTIAL FOR TREATMENT

Some people believe that money should not be wasted on attempts to treat or rehabilitate sex offenders. In 1993, the National Institutes of Mental Health spent more than $125 million for research on depression, but only about $1.2 million on research into the causes and treatments of sex offenses.[9]

Most experts agree that treatment of sex offenders is not very effective in preventing recidivism, that is, in preventing the offenders from repeating their abusive behavior. In the past, some experts believed that sex offenders did not usually commit new sex crimes.[10] But now it is generally thought that most of these offenses remain undetected, and that abusers usually offend again and again.

Some treatment programs show better results than others, but comparisons are difficult because standards vary from one program to another. For instance, a program dealing with hard-core, violent criminals will most likely have a lower success rate than one that selects abusers whose offenses are less serious. Regardless of the nature of their problems, antisocial individuals with little or no motivation to change are very poor candidates for any kind of therapy. In 1989, a review of studies of sex-offender programs revealed no evidence that treatment worked at all. Incarceration does not have much effect on behavior, but it is not clear that treatment works either, especially when it is mandatory.[11] Treatment programs in special prisons such as Avenel, in New Jersey, mentioned earlier, and in other facilities throughout the country, were cut back severely in the 1990s.

Treating sex offenders presents a number of problems. A large percentage of those in prison refuse all treatment. The murderer of Megan Kanka was one of those who had refused treatment while he was incarcerated at Avenel, and after serving a six-year sentence he was released without any kind of supervision or therapy.

Others appear to be sincere and cooperative with therapy, but only go through the motions, fooling even the most experienced therapists. Peter, for example, had been incarcerated for rape. He was discharged from the sex-offender treatment center on parole, but shortly afterward was sent back for violating his parole by committing another rape. Although there were witnesses, and his guilt was unmistakable, Peter steadfastly proclaimed his innocence for the next seven years. One day, he finally broke down and admitted to his prison therapist that he had indeed committed the rape, and had also raped six other young women while out on parole. In addition, he confessed to the rape and mur-

MYTH *Sex offenders choose victims of a race different from their own.*

FACT *Sex crimes are committed by people of all races, and generally, the victims are the same race as the offender.*

der of young girls and women years earlier during a massacre in Vietnam. He told the therapist that he had violated his parole so that he would be caught and sent back to prison; he thought he should be kept in prison for the rest of his life.[12]

Peter finally was able to admit his guilt, but many offenders never do so. They are reluctant to disclose the extent of their abusive behavior because they know they will be prosecuted. Sex offenders always tend to deny, minimize, make excuses, or tell only part of the story.

In some states, a person convicted of a sex offense may receive a longer prison sentence than someone who is convicted of murder. In prison, his life is worse than that of other inmates, because his crime places him on the lowest rung of the prison's social ladder.[13] Knowing the harsh punishments he may have to endure, a person may be afraid to tell the truth, which makes the task of evaluation and treatment more difficult.

Because offenders are unreliable about reporting what really happened, the expert who does the evaluation must obtain information from other sources such as the police, family, friends, witnesses, and victims.

Psychological tests and polygraph (lie detector) tests are also used.

In the past, sex offenders were dealt with by the criminal justice system; if they were found guilty of sexual abuse, they were sentenced to prison, and little was attempted in the way of rehabilitation.[14] However, not all abusers need to be incarcerated. Some can be treated in the community after they are carefully investigated and evaluated. Scott is a pleasant, attractive thirty-one-year-old real estate agent. He has just been released after serving his third prison term for sexual offenses. Over a period of eighteen years, he has molested more than two hundred boys. He admits that he is still attracted to young boys, and he thinks he will never be cured, but now he spends most of his time trying to avoid molesting children.

Scott is motivated to succeed in fighting his sexual addiction, and he attends weekly therapy sessions in a group that includes rapists and exhibitionists in addition to pedophiles. He does not leave his home or office when kids might be walking to or from school. He shuns television programs that involve handsome young male actors, and he avoids looking at pictures of boys in newspapers and magazines. He takes a medication that lowers his sex drive, and because he is a recovering alcoholic, he is tested every week to make sure that he does not drink. If Scott does not commit another sexual offense, he will be among the few for whom treatment seems to work.[15]

An individual who feels no remorse or guilt and thinks there is nothing wrong with his behavior is not suitable for treatment; experts agree that this kind of offender should be incarcerated, as he is dangerous and likely to continue abusing.[16] A person who acknowl-

CHAPTER FIVE

EFFECTS ON THE VICTIMS

Five-year-old Johanna was playing next door with her six-year-old friend Steve. Suddenly, Steve's mother heard her son calling her in a tearful voice, and she ran to the playroom to see what was wrong. What she saw shocked her. Johanna had undressed and was trying to take Steve's clothes off and telling him to lie on top of her. The incident was reported to the county social service department because Johanna's behavior was very unusual for a five-year-old child.

An investigation revealed that Johanna's parents had been asked to remove her from the preschool she had attended because of similar behavior there. At first, her parents said they did not know why Johanna was showing this behavior, but the investigators discovered that her father had been sexually abusing her. Her mother had been afraid to speak out against her husband for fear of arousing his bad temper.

Johanna acted in an extremely friendly and seductive manner with the male doctor who talked to her.

Asking for candy, she caressed him and tried to fondle his genitals. She later showed similar behavior with a foster brother and father in two different foster placements.[1] This kind of behavior is not unusual in children like Johanna, whose fathers started abusing them at an early age. They learn that sexy behavior earns affection and approval, so they continue it with other people.[2]

A very young child cannot understand why becoming involved in sexual activity with an adult is harmful, especially if the adult is trusted and has not been violent. One little girl asked why everyone was so upset about the sexual activity. She said those were the times when her father told her he loved her; no one cared when he pulled her hair or punched her.[3] The physical sensation of the activity may feel pleasurable; this is a normal reaction to stimulation of the genitals. In addition, the sense of closeness and affection are appealing. The offender may also have offered gifts or special privileges in order to manipulate the child into complying with the sexual behavior.

Johanna became very confused and upset when she discovered that other people rejected her for the very same behavior that her father encouraged and rewarded. Her father denied he had done anything harmful and he refused treatment; her mother did not want the marriage to break up. It was too risky to send Johanna back home, so she was placed with foster parents. This made Johanna feel worse; she thought her parents did not want her because she was bad and had done something wrong. Nobody seemed to want her or like her.

It is common for children to feel guilty and ashamed after they become aware of the feelings that

> **MYTH** *Seductive children are responsible for many sexual assaults.*
>
> **FACT** *No child is responsible for sexual assault by an adult. Children who show sexually aggressive behavior have learned the behavior from an abuser.*

others hold about sexual abuse. Then they feel responsible for the abusive behavior. After they disclose the abuse, they may also feel responsible for the consequences (such as the father having to leave home). This assumption of guilt and responsibility is sometimes called the "damaged goods syndrome."[4]

Children who are abused by their parents are more seriously affected than other victims because they feel betrayed by the very people they depend on for nurturance and protection. This can result in anger, depression, feelings of being alone, and an inability to trust other people or to form healthy relationships with them. Children who promised to keep the abuse a secret may also feel guilty about breaking the promise.

Johanna was fortunate. She went to live with an understanding foster family and received treatment that made her feel better about herself. She also realized that she was not responsible for what had happened, and she learned different, more appropriate, ways of expressing affection for others.

Inappropriate sexual behavior is only one of a number of symptoms that may be present in sexually abused children. The effects of sexual abuse are not fully understood, and are not the same in all cases. A few victims seem to escape any lasting effects, but most suffer serious problems.

THE SYMPTOMS AND AFTERMATH

More than three dozen studies have been done comparing sexually abused children with similar groups of children who have not been abused.[5] The results of these studies vary, partly because they use different definitions of abuse. Also, some studies do not distinguish between different kinds of abuse, some of which may be more damaging than others.

In addition, many abused children come from homes that are disturbed, chaotic, and violent. Sexual abuse is only one of several kinds of abuse these children suffer, and it is difficult to tell which problems were caused by the sexual abuse and which by other bad conditions in their homes.[6] Some studies have found that girls who have poor relationships with their mothers, or who have been separated from their mothers, appear to be at greater risk; however, it is possible that their difficult relationships with their mothers are the results of the sexual abuse as well as a risk factor.[7]

There are several variables that influence the nature and severity of the consequences of childhood sexual abuse: the age and sex of the victim, the sex of the offender, the relationship of the offender to the child, the nature of the abuse, its duration over a period of time, the use of physical force, family relationships, and the reactions of other people.[8] For example, the psychological consequences are probably worse if the offender is closely related to the child, if physical force is used, if the abuse is more severe (for example, intercourse), and if it occurs over a long period of time. Some experts believe that the consequences are more serious if the abuse occurs when the child is young.[9] Others believe that older children suffer worse after-effects.[10]

Psychological problems can show up at any time when a child has been abused sexually. Sometimes there are no symptoms until later in life, and in other instances an abused child may suddenly begin showing changes in behavior. Some common signs of abuse are: vague fears, feelings of being unprotected or helpless, nightmares, bedwetting, sleeping problems, fear of losing parents' love or approval, great need to please other people, poor self-esteem, anger, depression, withdrawal from activities, daydreaming, difficulty in concentrating, and behavior problems.

Girls who have been abused are more likely to show symptoms like depression, while boys are more likely to exhibit aggressive behavior.[11] In one study, teachers rated 36 percent of abused children as abnormally aggressive in class, in contrast to only 13 percent of a control group.[12]

Although many victims are boys, more attention has been given to female victims. Social workers and police officers tend to assume mistakenly that the abusive incident was only normal sex play among boys. Another reason is that blame is often placed on the victim rather than on the offender, especially in the case of boys. Many people believe that the incident would not have occurred if the boy had fought off his attacker. They think that the victim must be weak or a sissy, or wanted to engage in the sexual activity.

Ted is an eight-year-old boy who was stopped by a twelve-year-old neighbor boy who threatened him and made him perform a sex act. Ted was very frightened that the other boy would beat him up if he did not cooperate. When Ted told his parents, his father said that any "real man" would die before he did such a thing, and he accused Ted of being homosexual. In such a case, a boy can became confused and worried about his sexual identity, which is not unusual for a boy who is sexually abused by other boys or by men. Ted was afraid that his father was right. He began to wonder if his abuser chose him because he acted effeminate.

A boy may think he is homosexual if the sexual experience was at all pleasurable. On the other hand, if he is molested by a female and finds it distasteful, he may believe he is gay, because boys are supposed to like sex with females.[13] When parents or others refuse to believe the victim, make him feel ashamed, or call him homosexual, it increases his confusion and anxiety. It is not surprising that for these reasons, boys are less likely than girls to tell anyone about the abuse.

Many boys who were not aggressive before the sexual assault become aggressive afterward as a way of proving to themselves and others that they are not sissies. If they present themselves as tough, they can re-

MYTH *If a child does not resist an adult's sexual demands, it means that the child wants to participate in the activity.*

FACT *Compliance does not mean consent. Nothing gives offenders permission to sexually abuse a person.*

gain their masculine image and prevent others from taking advantage of them again. The aggressive behavior may include picking fights, destroying property, and disobeying rules at home and at school.

Boys who have been sexually abused are at risk of becoming sex offenders themselves. These boys try to undo their own victimization and regain their masculinity by doing to other children what was done to them. They may believe that they must choose between being a victim or being an abuser.

Adults who were physically or sexually abused in childhood are generally at a significantly higher risk of being arrested for committing crimes (including sex crimes) than those who were not abused. Experts believe that the criminal activities are due more to the stress of the childhood experiences than to the specific kind of abuse. Victims of childhood sexual abuse, however, are more likely to be arrested for prostitution than are victims of physical abuse. Studies have shown that men who were physically abused in childhood are more likely to commit rape than those who were abused or neglected in other ways. This finding is not surprising, in light of the fact that rape is primarily a crime of violence.[14]

One mother of a boy who was molested was afraid that her son would grow up to become a mass murderer. But not every abused child becomes a criminal or an abuser. With the help of therapy and education in parenting skills, most adults who were abused as children make a great effort to avoid abusing when they become parents.

In addition to confusion about sexual identity, victims of sexual abuse show other problems related to sexual feelings. Some children become preoccupied by thoughts about sex and may masturbate excessively. They may use sex as a means of showing affection or gaining approval, as Johanna did. Others may find sex repugnant and be unable to enjoy normal sexual relationships as adults.[15] According to Dr. Lenore Terr, some "sex survivors" fear falling under the influence of others such as teachers, friends, and lovers. They may experience psychosomatic aches and pains caused by emotional disturbance.[16]

Some experts believe that many symptoms found in victims of child abuse can be attributed to a disorder known as post-traumatic stress disorder (PTSD). In one study, the symptoms of PTSD were found in 44 percent of sexually abused children.[17] PTSD can result after any kind of experience or event that would be distressing for most people—for example, earthquakes or other natural disasters, kidnapping, and violent physical attacks, including rape and sexual assault. Those who suffer from this disorder are often irritable, edgy, easily startled by unexpected sounds, and may have problems sleeping and concentrating. When reminded of the traumatic experience, they may have flashbacks (recurring memories or feelings from the past), nightmares, and other distressing physical and emotional reactions. They may act or feel as though they are reliving the experience.

Individuals with PTSD avoid situations, people, and places that remind them of the traumatic event. They also try to avoid thoughts and feelings connected with it.[18] Some go through life feeling emotionally detached or numb. Their response is like building a dike to keep the bad memories from flooding in, but unwanted flashbacks break through again and again, bringing back the trauma.

While children are experiencing severe physical or sexual abuse, they often imagine they are somewhere else, or they pretend that the abuse is happening to another person. They may even induce a kind of hypnotic trance in themselves in order to escape the trauma. In this way, they are able to push the experience out of their consciousness.[19] If the trauma begins at an early age, and is severe and prolonged, it may later result in a condition known as multiple personality disorder (MPD), also called dissociative identity disorder. This is a condition in which there are two or more distinct personality states that take control of the person's thinking and behavior from time to time. Each personality is separate and has characteristics that are very different from the individual's main personality. The individual may not be aware of the other identities, and may not be able to remember what happened during the times the others were in control.[20]

Jessie grew up in an abusive family and was sexually molested by her stepfather from the time she was five years old until she reached her teens. She sometimes acted angry and aggressive, but at other times she was meek and shy, and her memory often appeared to have gaps; no one understood why her personality was so changeable. When she sought treatment as an adult, she described the sexual abuse and said that she used to "space out" while it was happening. She learned at an early age how to remove the traumatic event from her consciousness, and it became easier and easier for her to do this at will in order to escape. Since she could not escape physically, she escaped mentally. The result was that, by the time she was an adult, she had developed about forty distinct personalities, all with special talents, abilities, and characteristics.

Many adults in treatment for emotional problems are survivors of child abuse. Studies of patients in mental hospitals have shown that 20 to 50 percent were abused as children. In one study of adolescents who had been hospitalized because of mental illness and drug or alcohol addiction, 61 percent had been physically or sexually abused.[21]

TYPES OF THERAPY

Experts agree that making decisions about what is best for a victim of sexual abuse is a very difficult task. Each case is different, and there is no proven formula for treatment. A child who is an incest victim and who has suffered prolonged abuse is most likely in greater need of intensive therapy than one who was approached on one occasion by a nonviolent stranger. Both individual and group therapy are used, often along with assertiveness training, stress management, and, in some instances, hypnosis.

Most experts agree that group therapy is the most helpful type of therapy. Most victims feel very isolated, different from others, guilty, and ashamed. Often they cannot get rid of their feelings of being "damaged goods" until they have had a chance to exchange stories with others who have had similar experiences. Group members provide help and support for each other.

In the case of incest, not only the victim but the entire family needs treatment and support.[22] In many situations, difficult decisions have to be made by child protective services. For instance, some homes are so abusive that children must be removed permanently and then adopted by a stable family.

In 1985, the Support Program for Abuse Reactive Kids, known as SPARK, was established in Los

Angeles to treat children under the age of thirteen (most of whom had been abused) who were sexually abusing other children. This program provides group treatment for the children. Their parents also attend group sessions, where they receive support, parenting advice, and sex education.

The therapists at SPARK invented a unique kind of play therapy they call "monster therapy." The idea behind it is that their problem is a monster; the monster behavior is their compulsive, sexual acting-out behavior, which is represented by the use of puppets and stuffed animals. It is made clear to the children that they are not bad, but it is the monster behavior that is bad. The children are never called monsters. They learn that the behavior is something outside themselves that they can control, and the therapy and activities focus on conquering the monster. They are also taught to imagine how their victims felt; most of these children lack empathy for others. Sex education, social skills, assertiveness training, increasing self-esteem, and relapse prevention are other issues that are dealt with in therapy.[23]

CHAPTER SIX

GETTING AT THE TRUTH

In view of all the turmoil and stress that the revelation of abuse can cause, ignoring and forgetting the incident might appear to many people to be the easiest solution, especially in the case of incest. According to one estimate, only about 10 percent of sexual abuse cases are reported to the police or child protective services. One third of adult women who had been sexually molested as children said they had never told anyone about the abuse until they were asked in the course of a survey done by the *Los Angeles Times.* Most of those who had told someone said that no effective action had been taken.[1]

Child victims feel compelled by guilt or fear to keep the secret. If they do tell, they are sometimes persuaded by parents to retract their story in order to keep the family together. Retraction is very common, especially among victims of incest, because things often get worse for them instead of better after they reveal the abuse. Everyone blames them for the resulting disgrace and the breakup of the family; the offending father or stepfather may be removed from the home and faced with imprisonment; or the victim may be placed in foster care.

FALSE REPORTS

Experts agree that children rarely lie about sexual abuse; estimates of false allegations range from 1 to 10 percent of reported abuse cases.[2] False reports of abuse are sometimes elicited from young children under some circumstances, most likely during battles by parents over custody or visitation rights. The implanting of false memories has been used in many divorce cases where a child is convinced that the father was a sexual abuser and testifies to this. In one study of 18 children who had made such accusations in divorce battles, psychiatrists found that the majority of these children had given false reports.[3]

When there is pressure from an adult and leading questions are asked repeatedly about something a child

---

MYTH *All memories of sexual abuse must be true.*

FACT *Although many people have true memories of abuse that took place, sometimes a person may believe that thoughts and fantasies are memories of actual happenings.*

---

has said, eventually the child may believe that he or she was abused. Leading questions are those that contain the answer that the examiner wants, presented in a way that elicits that answer. Even when experts interview young children, they may come to wrong conclusions if they use leading questions or if they misinterpret something the child has said. One little girl complained that she did not like her father tickling her between the legs, and everyone assumed this was sexual abuse. But when another interviewer asked the child to describe it exactly, she said that her father tickled her around her knees.[4]

Children are more likely to deny an actual event that was upsetting than to make up false stories about events that did not happen. A study conducted with 75 children found that they reported correctly the actual facts about a scene they observed, but were influenced by the interviewer's suggestions concerning the interpretation of what they saw.[5] Since many sexually abused children are under the age of six, it is difficult to obtain proof of abuse unless there is a record of physical injury to the genital area.

It is often impossible to say with certainty whether or not abuse has actually occurred. If a child shows some of the psychological and behavioral problems described previously, it does not necessarily mean that he or she was sexually abused, because these symptoms can also have other causes. Physical proof is usually not present, but finding a sexually transmitted disease, or rectal or genital injury in a young child, indicates a high probability of abuse. Pregnancy, of course, is a certain indication.[6] Other possible indications that sexual abuse has occurred are urinary infections, unusual or offensive odors, and irritated or itchy genitals.

DIFFICULTIES IN INVESTIGATING

Investigation of abuse can be a very complicated process, upsetting and disruptive to the victim and family. It can involve physical examinations, numerous interviews with social workers, psychiatrists or psychologists, and law enforcement officers.

Young children cannot describe sexual abuse accurately because they lack the vocabulary, so interviewers may use dolls with male and female genitals, with which the children can demonstrate what happened. Dolls can be helpful in investigating sexual abuse, especially for children between the ages of two and six, but they are not acceptable as legal evidence. Doll play is another medium of communication, like language, but it is not necessarily a sure test, and experts disagree about its usefulness. For instance, a child who has not been abused, but who has witnessed adults having sexual relations or who has seen pornographic material, may make the dolls mimic the observed activity.[7] Drawings are another way that children can communicate what happened to them.

Testifying in court may also be a frightening and confusing experience for some children. Young children do not understand why so many different people ask them the same questions. Children may leave out important information that they have told another interviewer, because they think everyone already knows their story. The courtroom can be very scary, and some children believe that they are the ones who will be punished. One child expressed a fear that the judge would hit her with his "hammer," as she called his gavel.[8]

Experts recommend that child witnesses be prepared before testifying in order to lessen the children's stress. Some prosecutors take them on a tour of the courtroom beforehand and explain what is going to happen. Some locations have "court school" programs.

Studies have shown that testifying in court does not need to be a traumatic experience for most victims, especially if the professionals involved are trained to be aware of the special needs of children in these circumstances.[9] For example, a judge may make special rules concerning the attorneys' behavior in order to minimize any intimidation, such as not approaching too close to the child witness during questioning.[10] In some cases, children are allowed to testify from behind a screen or are videotaped with only the judge, attorneys, and the defendant in the room.

MEMORIES OF ABUSE: TRUE OR FALSE?

For many years, psychologists and psychiatrists have been conducting experiments to try to find out whether or not children's memories of abuse are reliable.[11] Children who have false memories often pick up details from television, newspapers, magazines, and suggestions from therapists.

Some adults who seek treatment for psychological problems have no recollection of having been molested as young children, but the memories may return during the course of treatment. In some cases, however, leading questions, hypnosis, or other techniques may unleash recollections of abuse that never occurred but that the person remembers as real. Researchers and therapists agree that traumatic memories can be forgotten and remembered in later years, but they also know that a memory can be suggested and then remembered as true.[12] However, people above the age of three do not seem to forget many things that are emotionally traumatic, such as repeated sexual abuse.[13]

The American Psychological Association says that repressed memories of child sexual abuse should not be taken at face value, but should not be dismissed as fantasy either.[14]

Sharon insists that she remembers lying in bed night after night listening for her father's steps in the hall. As they grew closer, she held her breath. She would watch the door, hoping it would not open. Sharon relives these thoughts over and over now that she is twenty and in therapy for bulimia, a condition in which she overeats and then forces herself to vomit. She is told that eating disorders can be connected with early child sexual assault.

Sharon did not remember the sexual abuse until her therapist asked again and again if her father might have abused her when she was a child. After she was questioned, the memories of the sexual abuse grew clearer. She hopes that learning what had been upsetting her through the years will make it possible for her to conquer her eating problem and begin a new life.

Sharon's therapist told her that it was common to repress memories of terrible experiences and that digging out these memories was essential for healing. After that, Sharon relived the nights of listening for the

---

MYTH *Anyone who has been sexually abused shows unmistakable signs of physical abuse.*

FACT *Often, there is no physical evidence of sexual abuse.*

---

steps in the hall. They seemed very real. After the old memories were loosened and after more sessions with her therapist, she felt certain she would be able to enjoy a new life.

Whether or not Sharon's memories are based on any truth is a complicated question, a question that is causing great controversy among therapists today. Thousands of adults have recovered bad memories in recent years.[15] As many as 60.7 percent of patients in a study at the Institute of Pennsylvania Hospital were able to document at least one episode of abuse that they had alleged in therapy.[16]

Starting in the 1980s, thousands of families received letters or calls from their adult children claiming to have recalled sexual abuse that took place years before. In some but not all cases, the sexual abuse really happened. In March 1992, a small group of accused families and concerned professionals formed the False Memory Syndrome Foundation to study the phenomenon and to help those affected by it. In only three and a half years, more than 17,000 people contacted the False Memory Syndrome Foundation to report that an adult in their family had suddenly "recovered repressed memories."[17]

Accepting the truth of long-forgotten memories elicited by therapy without corroboration can seriously injure and disrupt the lives of innocent family members.[18] It is not enough to have a feeling that something happened. There must be specific things that point to sexual abuse in the past, like confirmation from siblings, school or medical personnel, or others. Good therapists must help their patients to remember what really happened without using techniques that could encourage false memories.

According to the Philadelphia-based False Memory Syndrome Foundation, nearly 800 suits had been brought by children who accused family members of abuse recalled years later with the aid of a therapist. The 1994 publication of *The Myth of Repressed Memory* by Dr. Elizabeth Loftus began an outcry against therapists who help patients retrieve long-forgotten memories of sexual abuse.

Since the lifting of the statutes of limitations in many states, old crimes of sexual abuse can now be tried based on recalled memories. The first famous case in which a person recalled such a crime was one in which the abuse happened to a friend. In 1991, George Thomas Franklin was sentenced to life in prison after his daughter Eileen testified to memories of his raping and killing one of her friends twenty-two years earlier. However, the decision was overturned on a technicality in April 1995. On July 2, 1996, prosecutors said they would not retry Franklin because Eileen's sister testified that both she and Eileen had been hypnotized before the first trial. This brought the accuser's testimony into question.[19]

Some experts believe that the phenomenon of recovered memory is rare.[20] According to Janice Haaken, a psychologist who had studied the incest survivors' movement, what feels like a repressed memory often expresses the emotional, not the literal, truth of an experience. Some psychiatrists say that a patient might easily confuse dreams with memories if the patient is not being treated by a competent therapist.[21] While helping patients to recall memories can be an important part of therapy, people may take bits and fragments that are stored and use them to reconstruct a memory that makes sense to them now.

Adult memories of childhood sex abuse have sparked a heated debate. Dr. Judith Lewis Herman, a psychiatrist at Harvard Medical School, regards the new emphasis on adult memories of early sexual abuse as a healthy antidote to decades of legal and psychiatric neglect suffered by abused individuals.[22]

Another source of controversy in sexual abuse cases is the role of multiple personality disorder (MPD), in which a person manifests more than one identity. Do victims form multiple personalities as an extreme way of dissociating from the trauma of sexual abuse? As mentioned in Chapter Five, a child exposed to constant sexual assaults might deaden his or her pain by imagining that the abuse is happening to someone else, or might assign memories to an alternate self. This may play a part in the development of multiple personality disorder.

Many false memories, including tales of ritual abuse, are reported by patients who suffer from MPD. Some of these appear to spring from fantasies, accord-

MYTH *People who suffer from conditions such as multiple personality disorder or post-traumatic stress disorder must have been sexually abused as children, even if they do not remember the abuse.*

FACT *A variety of psychological problems can cause these disorders.*

ing to George Ganaway, a psychiatrist at Emory University School of Medicine, and others. Still other psychiatrists view incest as a key influence on most cases of MPD.[23]

Certainly, the number of reported cases of multiple personality disorder has risen dramatically since the beginning of the century. Patients may have from two or three personalities to as many as a hundred. The increase in reported cases may be due to greater awareness of the disease, but some experts believe that in many cases the condition may first exist in the minds of therapists. These therapists then diagnose MPD in highly suggestible individuals.

Distinguishing genuine incest victims from those who have false memories is a serious problem. More than 400,000 reports of verifiable sexual assaults are filed with authorities each year by teachers and doctors who work with obviously battered and traumatized children.[24] The most serious danger presented by false accusations may be that the true accusations will be discredited.[25]

Recently, researchers have studied scans of the brain when it goes awry and brings up false memories. In this new research, led by Dr. Daniel Schacter of Harvard University, false memories can be clearly distinguished from those that are true. There are still many questions about the reliability and limitations of this new technique. At present, the testing method is too complicated and expensive to use in cases of sexual abuse to determine whether or not repressed memories are true.

In his book *Searching for Memory: The Brain, The Mind, and The Past,* Dr. Schacter summarizes the current scientific evidence concerning the accuracy of recovered memories of childhood sexual abuse: "There are a few well-documented cases, but little scientific credible information is available."[26]

MEDIA AND MASS HYSTERIA

The controversy over the validity of memories of childhood sexual abuse has raised many critical issues. Some experts believe that the issue of repressed or suggested memories of abuse has been overreported and sensationalized by the news media. Long-buried memories of sexual abuse are popular subjects on afternoon television talk shows. The subject has found its way into the headlines of newspapers and magazines, into living rooms, movies, and courtrooms. Celebrities such as Oprah Winfrey and La Toya Jackson have talked publicly about their anguish and healing. In 1991, television actress Roseanne Barr Arnold told the media a story of her abuse by her mother from infancy to the age of seven. Former Miss America Marilyn Van Derbur told the world that she had been sexually abused by her father and repressed the memory until she was twenty-four years old.[27]

In 1995, three of the Dionne quintuplets, who were famous in the 1930s as the first quintuplets on record to survive more than a few days, accused their father of sexual abuse. Other family members deny this charge, but the three siblings claim that they had to speak up to find "inner peace" and liberate themselves from the past.[28]

Cases of recovered memories have made many headlines. Although there have been cases of child sexual abuse in day-care centers, many of these appear to have been built on hysteria and false memories. Some of these cases have been compared to the Salem witch hunts

MYTH *Children and adolescents make up stories about sexual abuse.*

FACT *This is extremely unlikely. Even if children change their stories upon repeated questioning, it does not mean they are lying. Reporting sexual abuse is an unpleasant experience, and the same questions must be answered many times. Especially in the case of incest, parents may persuade a child to retract what he or she has said. It is also possible for interviewers to mislead or confuse a young child.*

that took place in colonial New England. Many people were convicted on the words of children and experts who spoke for them.

In the 1980s, there was a wave of "satanic ritual abuse" trials, which included tales of devil worship, pornography, and murder. The sensationalized press coverage has led many people to believe that there is a nationwide network of satanic groups preying on the young, but the extent of the problem is greatly exaggerated. Individuals and couples who claim to be involved in the worship of Satan have included some children in ritual abuse practices, but the majority of the tales are unsupported. In a survey conducted for the National Center on Child Abuse and Neglect, researchers found more than 12,000 accusations of ritual sexual abuses by satanic cults. Investigators were not able to substantiate any of them.[29]

Some people use the probable false memories of satanic sexual abuse to cast doubt on all memories of abuse; others find stories of cult sexual abuse easier to believe that those of incest. In *Rocking the Cradle of Sexual Politics*, author Louise Armstrong states that the uproar over satanic ritual abuse, along with emphasis on false memories, may succeed in casting suspicion on the entire issue of real incest.[30]

CHAPTER SEVEN

REDUCING THE RISK OF SEXUAL ABUSE

Cassidy learned to tell the difference between good and bad touching when she was in kindergarten. Her school had coloring books, puppet shows, plays, and songs about sexual abuse, and she knew just what she would do if someone threatened her. While education about abuse has been very successful with some very young children, for others it is confusing.

Alyssa remembers the days when her parents warned her about bad touches and cautioned her to be aware of strangers. They fussed so much about it that when she was seven years old, she was afraid to answer questions from any stranger, even a salesperson. She thought all men that she did not know might try to lure her, kidnap her, and sexually abuse her. Even though she knows now that most people are not going to abduct her, she is still cautious about strangers. But she remembers being confused about what some of the stories concerning good and bad touches actually meant.[1]

Programs that emphasize the danger of abuse by strangers often ignore the more common problem of abuse by acquaintances and family members. There are children who grow up unaware that they need not subject themselves to sexual abuse by their own fathers. Other educational programs that give children the message to "just say no" are also inadequate. Since children cannot control adults, this approach may just succeed in making children feel guilty for not stopping the adult who forces abuse on them.

The best programs help children to feel free to tell a trusted adult what has happened. In one study by David Finkelhor, a psychologist and expert on the subject of child abuse, two thirds of 2,000 children reported attending a program about abuse or how to prevent being a victim. Of the children who were interviewed, 115 cited cases of attempted or completed sexual abuse. These children showed definite benefits from the programs, including a much greater willing-

---

MYTH *It's not important for children to know about sexual abuse.*

FACT *Knowing about sexual abuse helps to prevent it. It is as important for children to know about sexual assault for their own safety as it is for them to know about fire safety, traffic safety, and water safety. Children who have inadequate information about sexual abuse are less apt to report it and seek help.*

ness to disclose episodes to someone else. Children who had instruction from their parents as well as at school were even more likely to benefit.

As a result of the study, it was concluded that abuse prevention programs may need to do more to teach children how to avoid physical injury during a sexual assault.[2] Most of the programs outline the basic steps for children to take if someone attempts to abuse them sexually. Many programs suggest that children do the following:

1. Say "No" (or something else, such as "Don't do that," "I don't want to," or "I'm going to tell on you if you don't stop").
2. Tell someone who you trust and is old enough to help you.
3. Keep telling until someone believes you and helps you.
4. Remember that the attack is not your fault.

While there is no perfect way to protect against sexual abuse, young people need to be aware of behavior that does not seem right—for example, if someone stands or sits too close, grabs or pushes to get his or her way, restricts someone else from leaving, or acts more intimately than the other person wants. The person being harassed should respond immediately, without being concerned about hurting feelings or being rude.

The sexual abuse and exploitation of children is a silent, growing epidemic. Preventing it is everybody's problem. Older children can help by teaching younger kids what the limits should be and how to be assertive when someone assaults them or gives signs of planning to do so. Adults should teach children how to try to prevent sexual abuse, and the importance of reporting any abusive behavior. Discussions in schools and at home might help young people understand that someone who attacks a child is motivated by sexual attraction, anger, powerlessness, and a need for control—feelings he responds to by attacking someone weaker.

THE NEED FOR NEW THINKING

There must be deterrents in place to prevent children from being victimized, and some experts suggest that society make a greater effort to stress the fact that it is unacceptable to sexually abuse children. Television, music, movies, and advertising send messages that glamorize sexual aggression and degrade women. Dr. Peter Scales, of the Center for Early Adolescence of the University of North Carolina, reports that there is a small but alarming number of young people who do not regard sex abuse as a criminal act. He also notes that a surprising percentage of young women believe that a father or a boyfriend has the right to force himself on them sexually.[3]

Females who have been taught to be polite, accommodating, and nurturing exhibit traits that sexual offenders seek in a girl victim. Fortunately, most females today are taught to feel independent and to say no to something that seems wrong. Even in their own families, many young women realize that any extra attention and closeness that is a "secret" is wrong. They know that their bodies are their own property.

Although abusers are sometimes female, it is generally acknowledged that most abuse is committed by males, and the abusive behavior usually involves the use of power or force. If sexual abuse is to be prevented, or even decreased, the way many men feel about women in general needs to be changed. This change should begin when males are very young. Exposing one's body and peeping in a window while someone is undressing or involved in sexual acts are types of behavior that can in children be quite innocent, the result of normal curiosity about sexuality. But in some individuals, these childhood behaviors lead later to more serious sexual aggression, such as sexual assault and rape.[4]

There is a trend toward sex and violence at an earlier age, according to the Kempe National Center for Prevention and Treatment of Child Abuse and Neglect at the University of Colorado Health Center in Denver. This center maintains a national data base of 800 programs across the country, and in many of the programs there are offenders under the age of ten. About 400 started sexually abusing children before the age of twelve.[5]

The study entitled *Rape in America* revealed that 32 percent of all rapes involved young women between the ages of eleven and seventeen. Many of these rapes occurred while the young women were on dates.[6]

Recently, an increasing number of children have been attacking others in groups. For example, seven teens were accused of sexually attacking two fourteen-year-old girls, one of whom said she had been gang-raped three times. One time the rape took place in a school stairwell.

In another case, eight children, ages nine to thirteen, threw a twelve-year-old on the ground, held her down, and fondled her on a school playground. Such attacks are not uncommon, but in this case, six of the assaulters were girls.

Children who abuse other children are assumed to be victims imitating their attackers, but this is not always the case. While the leaders of group attacks are probably children who have been abused, peer pressure and cultural messages draw in other children.[7]

Some young people feel it is hard to draw a line between flirting and harassment, advances and abuse. For many boys, courting has become a game of abuse. In a nationwide survey of high school and junior high students, a large number of boys and girls said they had been groped, grabbed, and subjected to sexually explicit put-downs in school hallways. Many felt that it was "no big deal." But some said teenage dating has become scary. Although the vast majority of boys are not sex offenders, a growing number seem to view harassment as a game and abuse as a team sport.[8]

Early in 1993, a group of boys in Lakewood, California, who called themselves the Spur Posse, forced girls to have sex with them and kept score of their sexual conquests. Although the boys claimed that some of the girls "asked for it," they believed that their sexual abuse of the girls made them "all man."[9] Some of their parents did not see anything wrong with what they were doing, but letters from all over the country made it clear that most people felt that what the boys did was very wrong.

Helping young boys to respect the opposite sex is one step in breaking the cycle of sexual abuse. Although many parents have made significant changes in the way that they raise their daughters, encouraging them to respect themselves and to aspire to a wide choice of careers, they often continue to tolerate boys' language and behavior that demean girls. However, an increasing number of young people are becoming aware that boys can be courageous, strong, adventurous, sensitive, caring, and responsible without feeling the need to be tough, violent, or indulge in unfeeling behavior that is focused on power and dominance.[10]

CHAPTER EIGHT

WHAT YOU CAN DO

If you have been sexually abused, you may feel that no one can help you. You probably feel helpless, fearful, and angry. This is a normal way to feel if you have been abused. But there are some things you can and should do, even if they are difficult.

The one thing you should not do is blame yourself. Although each case of abuse is different, one fact is always the same: Sexual abuse is never your fault. It is the fault of the person who abused you. That person is to blame. He or she has broken the law.

Seek help by telling truthfully exactly what has happened to you. Tell someone who cares about you and someone you trust. That person should be old enough to help.

You may wish to talk about the problem with a parent first. Choose a time when no one else is around and you can get that parent's full attention. Suggest that there is something the two of you need to talk about and that you need help. Sometimes the parent will understand, but in many cases it is difficult for a parent to believe that the abuse has been happening, particularly if the abuser is a spouse or other family member. A mother, for example, may see the father in a different light or may be afraid of losing her home and source of income. Or she herself may be suffering from abuse by the same individual. Perhaps she was sexually abused when she was a child, and she accepts the abuse as a part of family life. A parent may refuse to believe you at first, partly because he or she hopes that if it is ignored the whole problem will go away.

If the first person you tell does not believe you, tell someone else until you find someone who will believe you and help. You might choose a teacher, a school counselor or principal, a grandparent, an aunt or uncle, an adult friend, or any other adult you feel will help. If you cannot find an adult person who can help you, call one of the hotlines listed at the end of this chapter.

The person you confide in may then consult a social worker or child protection worker. It is possible that you may be separated from the abuser for a period of time. In some states, the policy is to remove a sexually abused child from the home immediately and place him or her in a foster home or juvenile center temporarily. This separation of abuser and victim allows time for the abuser to get help for his or her problems so that you can feel safe and certain that the abuse will not continue. Many abusers hate themselves for what they are doing and are grateful for help in stopping their behavior.

Many organizations have counselors who will talk with you, your parents, and any other person involved in the abuse. They will seek every way they can to protect you, keep the family together, and avoid the abuser's arrest, if that is what you want.

You may be concerned that your abuser will learn that you have shared the "secret" with someone else. Most rape-crisis centers and child protection agencies keep all their cases confidential. Ask about their policy before you give your name.

In many parts of the country, there are people who belong to an organization known as CASA. They are Court Appointed Special Advocates who volunteer to help children in court and to take a special interest in their problems. They telephone and visit families, gathering information to help social workers and judges to decide what is best for a child. They also work with therapists, foster parents, and lawyers to help find the best solutions to a child's problems.

HELPING OTHERS

You can help by learning about and supporting abuse prevention organizations in your community and making others aware of them, perhaps by putting brochures in your library. Some groups provide posters for community bulletin boards. There are also some Internet sources for information about sexual abuse.

The Paul and Lisa Program, Inc., in Essex, Connecticut, fights child sexual exploitation by going directly to the streets to reach young prostitutes. It offers them transitional housing, counseling, job training, life-skills training, and a structured routine to help them to return to mainstream society. This group makes presentations about child sexual abuse to schools, civic clubs, citizen action groups, and others. Perhaps there is a group in your community that will provide a speaker for your school. Consult the local phone book or child

In Case of Rape

A rape victim should try to memorize as many physical details about the rapist as possible—the color of eyes and hair, height and weight, scars, tattoos, type of car, or anything else that is unusual. These details may help the police identify the attacker.

Each case is different. A victim may be paralyzed with terror and unable to resist the attack, or may fear that resistance could be fatal. Yelling, shouting, or fighting back may not always be wise. Some rapists may react to resistance with more violence. A victim may also try to win the attacker's sympathy and disrupt the rapist's fantasy.

After a rape, the victim should say whatever is necessary in order to get away from the attacker. For example, the victim should try to convince the rapist that he or she will not tell the police, and prefers just to forget what has happened.

Once free, the victim should immediately call a rape-crisis hotline, the police, a trusted friend, and a lawyer as soon as possible. Calling 911 will help the victim reach the police and a hotline. A victim should not bathe, shower, or clean his or her clothes before doctors and police have had a chance to gather evidence.

Being raped is a traumatic experience, physically and emotionally. Reporting a rape helps a victim take charge of life again. The victim will need medical help and counseling to work through anger, pain, and many other feelings. Friends cannot fully understand the effects of such a traumatic experience, but their support is important, too.

protection agency to ask how cases are handled in your area.

Most runaways have been abused at home, and running away simply puts them at great risk for abuse on the streets. Encourage a friend who wants to run away to call a hotline, such as the National Runaway Switchboard (1-800-621-4000) or the Boys Town National Hotline (1-800-448-3000), where confidential help is available.

Support the rape crisis clinic in your community by making people aware of it through letters to the editor, fund-raisers, and help from other community or religious groups.

You can also help simply by listening sympathetically when a friend tells you about an abusive situation. Be understanding—it is not easy for a victim of sexual abuse to talk about it. Let your friend know that you want to listen and that you care about what has happened. Realize that your friend has taken a risk in confiding in you, and needs your support. Believe what your friend tells you, even though you may be confused about some of the details. Do not blame your friend for what has happened, and do not talk to others about it. Most important, encourage and help your friend to report the abuse to someone in a position to help.

Chapter Nine

Where to Get Help

School counselors or school nurses can help you find services in your community for help in stopping an abusive situation. In addition to the following national organizations, local mental health clinics, rape crisis clinics, and child protective services may be helpful, too.

ORGANIZATIONS

American Humane Society
Child Protection Division
P.O. Box 1266
Denver, CO 80201-1266
Phone: 303-695-0811

False Memory Syndrome Foundation
3401 Market Street, Suite 130
Philadelphia, PA 19104-3315
Phone: 215-387-1865

National Center for Missing and
    Exploited Children
2101 Wilson Boulevard, Suite 550
Arlington, VA 22201-3052
Phone: 703-235-3900
HOTLINE: 800-843-5678
TDD (teletype device for the deaf): 800-826-7653

National Clearinghouse on Child Abuse
    and Neglect
U.S. Department of Health and Human Services
P.O. Box 1182
Washington, D.C. 20013-1182
Phone: 1-800-FYI-3366

National Crime Prevention Council
1700 K Street, NW, 2nd Floor
Washington, D.C. 20006
Phone: 202-466-6272

National Committee to Prevent
    Child Abuse (NCPCA)
P.O. Box 2866
Chicago, IL 60690
Phone: 1-800-55-NCPCA

HOTLINES

Local Crisis Hotline: Check your phone book on the
page listing community services.

Boys Town National Hotline:
1-800-448-3000

National Child Abuse Hotline (operated by
    Childhelp USA/IOF Foresters):
1-800-422-4453 or 1-800-4-A-CHILD.

National Runaway Switchboard:
1-800-621-4000.

Nine Line (operated by Covenant House):
1-800-999-9999.

National Center for Missing and Exploited Children:
1-800-843-5678

NOTES

CHAPTER ONE

1. "Child Sexual Abuse," Brochure (American Academy of Child and Adolescent Psychiatry, Mental Health Net, Internet 1995, 1996).
2. Sandy Wurtele and Cindy Miller-Perrin, *Preventing Child Sexual Abuse* (Lincoln: University of Nebraska Press, 1992), 12.
3. Barbara Lonnborg, "Abused Adolescents" (NE: Boys Town).
4. "Questions and Answers About Memories of Childhood Abuse" (Washington, D.C.: American Psychological Association, August 1995), 2.
5. Fact Sheet (Chicago: National Committee to Prevent Child Abuse, 1995).
6. Mic Hunter, editor, *Child Survivors and Perpetrators of Sexual Abuse: Treatment Innovations* (Thousand Oaks, CA: Sage, 1995), 88.
7. "Men Also Suffer Consequences of Childhood Abuse," *The Menninger Letter,* January 1995, 3.
8. Louise Armstrong, *Rocking the Cradle of Sexual Politics: What Happened When Women Said Incest* (Reading, MA: Addison Wesley, 1994), 9-10.

9. Debra Whitcomb, *When the Victim Is a Child* (Washington, D.C.: Department of Justice, 1992), 2.

10. Ronald M. Holmes, *Sex Crimes* (Newbury Park, CA: Sage, 1991), 83.

11. *Boy Scout Handbook*. Tenth Edition (Irving, TX: Boy Scouts of America, 1990), 530.

CHAPTER TWO

1. Diane H. Schetky and Arthur H. Green, *Sexual Abuse: A Handbook for Professionals* (New York: Bruner/Mazel, 1988), 29.

2. Gertrude Williams and John Money. *Traumatic Abuse and Neglect of Children at Home* (Baltimore: The Johns Hopkins University Press, 1980), 18.

3. Florence Rush, *The Best Kept Secret: The Sexual Abuse of Children* (Englewood Cliffs, NJ: Prentice-Hall, 1981), 27.

4. Ibid., 20-22.

5. Ibid., 23.

6. Williams and Money, *Traumatic Abuse and Neglect*, 17.

7. Schetky and Green, *Sexual Abuse*, 24.

8. Boswell, John. *The Kindness of Strangers: The Abandonment of Children in Western Europe from Late Antiquity to the Renaissance* (New York: Pantheon Books, 1988), 113.

9. Williams and Money, *Traumatic Abuse and Neglect*, 17.

10. Ibid., 17-18.

11. Rush, *The Best Kept Secret*, 65.

12. Schetky and Green, *Sexual Abuse*, 25.

13. C. Henry Kempe and Ray E. Helfer, *The Battered Child* (Chicago: University of Chicago Press, 1980), 18.

14. Rush, *The Best Kept Secret*, 64-66.

15. *Christian Science Monitor*, September 6, 1994.

16. Schetky and Green, *Sexual Abuse*, 29.

17. *Christian Science Monitor*, September 14, 1995.

18. Schetky and Green, *Sexual Abuse*, 157.

19. *Newsweek*, September 25, 1995, 62.

Chapter Three

1. Lorraine Waterhouse, editor, *Child Abuse and Child Abusers: Protection and Prevention* (London and Philadelphia: Jessica Kingsley Publishers, 1993), 114.
2. Mic Hunter, editor, *Child Survivors and Perpetrators of Sexual Abuse: Treatment Innovations* (Thousand Oaks, CA: Sage, 1995), 89.
3. Richard Layman, *Current Issues, Vol. 1: Child Abuse* (Detroit: Omnigraphics, Inc., 1990), 117.
4. Ronald M. Holmes, *Sex Crimes* (Newbury Park, CA: Sage, 1991), 36, 37.
5. *The Harvard Mental Health Letter*, Vol. 9, No. 11, May 1993, 2, 3.
6. Waterhouse, *Child Abuse*, 119.
7. Holmes, *Sex Crimes*, 41.
8. Ruth S. Kempe and C. Henry Kempe, *The Common Secret: Sexual Abuse of Children and Adolescents* (New York: W. H. Freeman and Company, 1984), 48.
9. William E. Prendergast, *Treating Sex Offenders in Correctional Institutions and Outpatient Clinics* (New York: The Haworth Press, Inc., 1991), 142, 143.
10. *The Harvard Mental Health Letter*, Vol. 9, No. 11, May 1993, 3.
11. Ibid.
12. Prendergast, *Treating Sex Offenders*, 5.
13. Hunter, *Child Survivors*, 92.
14. Ibid., 83, 111, 112.
15. Ibid., 80.
16. Ibid., 101.
17. Holmes, *Sex Crimes*, 34.

Chapter Four

1. *The New York Times*, May 10, 1996.
2. *The New York Times*, May 18, 1996.
3. *The New York Times*, February 2, 1995.

4. *The New York Times*, February 27, 1995.
5. *The New York Times*, February 28, 1995.
6. *The New York Times*, July 9, 1996.
7. *The New York Times*, February 27, 1995.
8. *U.S. News & World Report*, September 19, 1994, 68, 73.
9. Ibid., 74.
10. Holmes, *Sex Crimes*, 108.
11. *The New Yorker*, September 4, 1995, 61.
12. Prendergast, *Treating Sex Offenders*, 114.
13. Lenore E. A. Walker, editor, *Handbook on Sexual Abuse of Children* (New York: Springer Publishing Company, 1988), 219.
14. Schetky and Green, *Child Sexual Abuse*, 142.
15. *U.S. News & World Report*, September 19, 1994, 65, 67.
16. Walker, *Handbook on Sexual Abuse*, 370.
17. Prendergast, *Treating Sex Offenders*, 105.
18. *The Harvard Mental Health Letter*, Vol. 10, No. 1, July 1993, 4.
19. Adele Mayer, *Sex Offenders: Approaches to Understanding and Management* (Holmes Beach, FL: Learning Publications, 1988), 111, 112.
20. Holmes, *Sex Crimes*, 113.
21. Mayer, *Sex Offenders*, 116.
22. Ibid., 117.
23. *The Harvard Mental Health Letter*, Vol. 10, No. 1, July 1993, 4.
24. Schetky and Green, *Child Sexual Abuse*, 196.

CHAPTER FIVE

1. Kempe, *The Common Secret*, 56.
2. Ibid., 54, 55.
3. Layman, *Current Issues*, 44.
4. Kathleen Coulborn Faller, *Child Sexual Abuse: Intervention and Treatment Issues* (Washington, D.C.: Department of Health and Human Services, U.S. Department of Children and Families, 1993), 19.

5. Ibid., 18.

6. *The Harvard Mental Health Letter*, Vol. 9, No. 12, June 1993, 1.

7. Ann Wolbert Burgess, editor, *Child Trauma 1: Issues and Research* (New York: Garland Publishing, Inc., 1992), 336.

8. Jon R. Conte, *A Look at Child Sexual Abuse* (Chicago: National Committee to Prevent Child Abuse, 1986), 22, 23.

9. *The Harvard Mental Health Letter*, Vol. 9, No. 12, June 1993, 1.

10. Conte, *A Look at Child Sexual Abuse*, 22.

11. Walker, *Handbook on Sexual Abuse*, 81.

12. *The Harvard Mental Health Letter*, Vol. 9, No. 12, June 1993, 3.

13. Layman, *Current Issues*, 43.

14. Cathy Spatz Widom, *Victims of Childhood Sexual Abuse— Later Criminal Consequences* (Research in Brief, March 1995, National Institute of Justice), 2-7.

15. Faller, *Child Sexual Abuse*, 19.

16. Lenore Terr, *Unchained Memories: True Stories of Traumatic Memories Lost and Found* (New York: Basic Books, 1994), 172.

17. *The Harvard Mental Health Letter*, Vol. 9, No. 12, June 1993, 1, 2.

18. *Diagnostic and Statistical Manual of Mental Disorders, Fourth Edition* (Washington, D.C.: American Psychiatric Association, 1994), 424.

19. *The Harvard Mental Health Letter*, Vol. 9, No. 12, June 1993, 2.

20. *Diagnostic and Statistical Manual of Mental Disorders, Fourth Edition* (Washington, D.C.: American Psychiatric Association, 1994), 84.

21. *The Harvard Mental Health Letter*, Vol. 9, No. 12, June 1993, 3.

22. *The Harvard Mental Health Letter*, Vol. 10, No. 1, July 1993, 2, 3.

23. Hunter, *Child Survivors*, 68, 69.

CHAPTER SIX

1. *The Harvard Mental Health Letter,* Vol. 9, No. 12, June 1993, 3, 4.
2. Ibid., 4.
3. *The New York Times,* September 10, 1995.
4. Layman, *Current Issues,* 48.
5. Faller, *Child Sexual Abuse,* 53.
6. Ibid., 22.
7. Ibid., 46.
8. Debra Whitcomb, *When the Victim Is a Child* (Washington, D.C.: Department of Justice, 1992), 18.
9. Ibid., 28.
10. Ibid., 154.
11. Lenore Terr, *Unchained Memories: True Stories of Traumatic Memories Lost and Found* (New York: Basic Books, 1994), 168.
12. *The New York Times,* April 8, 1994.
13. *Insight,* October 23, 1993, 19.
14. *The New York Times,* November 15, 1994.
15. *Time,* April 17, 1995, 54-55.
16. *Psychology Today,* January/February 1996, 78.
17. *Forgotten Memory Syndrome Foundation Newsletter,* January 1996, 14.
18. Fred Frankel, "Discovering New Memories in Psychotherapy," *New England Journal of Medicine,* Vol. 333, No. 9, 591.
19. *The New York Times,* July 3, 1996.
20. "Questions and Answers About Memories of Childhood Abuse" (Washington, D.C.: American Psychological Association, August 1995), 1.
21. *The New York Times,* December 5, 1993.
22. *Science News,* September 18, 1993, 184.
23. *Science News,* September 18, 1995.
24. *Time,* April 17, 1995, 54-55.
25. *Harvard Mental Health Newsletter,* Vol. 11, No. 9, March 1995.

26. Daniel Schacter, *Searching for Memory: The Brain, The Mind, and The Past* (NY: Basic Books, 1996), 267.
27. *Harvard Mental Health Newsletter,* Vol. 9, No. 9, March, 1993, 4-5.
28. *The New York Times,* September 26, 1995.
29. *The New York Times,* October 31, 1994.
30. Armstrong, *Rocking the Cradle of Sexual Politics,* 257-258.

CHAPTER SEVEN

1. Hunter, *Child Survivors,* 89.
2. *Science News,* October 9, 1993, 231.
3. *The New York Times,* July 5, 1995.
4. Ibid., July 7, 1993.
5. Ibid., July 5, 1993.
6. "Rape in America: A Report to the Nation," Pamphlet (Arlington, VA: National Victim Center and Crime Victims Research and Treatment Center, April 1992).
7. *The New York Times,* July 5, 1993.
8. Ibid., July 17, 1995.
9. Ibid., March 29, 1993.
10. Ibid., July 21, 1994.

GLOSSARY

Child sexual abuse: Any physical contact or activity with a child that the child does not understand and cannot give informed consent to, and that is done for the gratification of the abuser. The abuser may be an adult or another child.

Compulsion: Repetitive behavior that a person feels driven to perform.

Damaged goods syndrome: Loss of self-esteem, feelings of worthlessness, poor self-image; sense of having been spoiled or damaged experienced by victims of sexual abuse.

Empathy: Ability to understand the feelings of another person.

Exhibitionist: Someone who receives sexual gratification from the deliberate exposure of private body parts to strangers.

Hebephile: A pedophile attracted to children who are past puberty.

Incest: Sexual molestation of a child by someone closely related by blood or marriage, or someone in a social relationship where he or she could be broadly defined as family. Incest does not always involve children.

Indecent exposure: Inappropriate exposure of the body; exhibitionism.

Obsession: Repetitive thought or impulse that is intrusive and not under a person's control.

Pedophile: Someone who is sexually attracted to children, generally those who have not reached puberty.

Pornography: Photographs, movies, videos, books, or other visual or printed material created for the purpose of arousing sexual feelings.

Prostitute: A person who exchanges sexual services for money.

Rape: Forced intercourse with an unwilling partner.

Recidivism: Tendency to revert to former behavior, especially criminal behavior.

Sadist: Someone who receives gratification from inflicting pain or humiliation on others.

Sibling: Brother or sister.

Sociopath: Person with an antisocial personality—that is, someone who behaves in ways not acceptable to society, with no feelings of guilt or remorse; someone who does not conform to society's definitions of what is right and wrong.

Virgin: A person who has not engaged in sexual intercourse.

Voyeur: Someone who receives sexual gratification from watching others (peeping), usually strangers, who are undressing, naked, or engaged in sexual activity.

FURTHER READING

Booher, Dianna Daniels. *Rape: What Would You Do?* New York: Messner, 1991.

Cooley, Judith. *Coping with Sexual Abuse.* New York: Rosen, 1991.

Goldentyer, Debra. *Family Violence.* Austin, TX: Raintree, 1995.

Hyde, Margaret O. *Know About Abuse.* New York: Walker, 1992.

———. *Sexual Abuse: Let's Talk About It.* Louisville, KY: Westminster/John Knox, 1987.

Johnson, Joan J. *Teen Prostitution.* New York: Franklin Watts, 1992.

LaValle, John. *Everything You Need to Know When You Are the Male Survivor of Rape or Sexual Assault.* New York: Rosen, 1996.

Mather, Cynthia L. *How Long Does It Hurt?* New York: Jossey-Bass, 1994.

Silverstein, Herma. *Date Abuse.* Springfield, NJ: Enslow, 1994.

Spies, Karen Bornemann. *Everything You Need to Know About Incest.* New York: Rosen, 1992.

Stark, Evan. *Everything You Need to Know About Sexual Abuse.* New York: Rosen, 1993.

Wekesser, Carol, and Karin L. Swisher. *Sexual Harassment.* New York: Greenhaven, 1992.

INDEX